MW00915486

MARIE CURIE

BOOK FOR CURIOUS KIDS

Exploring the Fascinating Life and Legacy of the First Woman to Win a Nobel Prize

ERIC LYLANI

ERIC LYLANI

TABLE OF CONTENTS

INTRODUCTION

Have you ever wondered what it would be like to discover something that changed the world forever? Imagine finding elements so powerful that they emit rays of light all on their own. What if I told you that a brilliant scientist named Marie Curie did just that?

Marie Curie's life was a tapestry of courage, curiosity, and discovery. She was not only the first woman to win a Nobel Prize but also the first person to win it twice in two different scientific fields! Her journey from a small town in Poland to the bustling streets of Paris is a story of resilience and determination.

Let's embark on an exciting adventure through Marie Curie's life. From her early days in Warsaw to her groundbreaking discoveries with her beloved husband Pierre, this book will take you on a captivating journey of scientific exploration and personal triumph.

Join me as we unravel the mysteries of Marie Curie's world and discover how her legacy continues to inspire generations of scientists and thinkers. Get ready to explore her life, her discoveries, and the lasting impact she made on the world. Are you ready to dive into the incredible story of Marie Curie? Let's begin!

Marie's Early Days in Warsaw

Once upon a time, in the bustling city of Warsaw, a little girl named Maria Skłodowska was born on November 7, 1867. Maria was the youngest of five children born to Bronisława and Władysław Skłodowski, who were both respected teachers. Maria's family had a rich history of fighting for Poland's independence, but this also meant they faced many challenges.

Maria, often called Mania by her family, grew up with her siblings Zofia (Zosia), Józef (Józio), Bronisława (Bronia), and Helena (Hela). Their family had endured hardship because of their involvement in Polish national uprisings. These struggles meant that Maria and her siblings had to work hard to succeed in life.

Maria's father, Władysław Skłodowski, taught mathematics and physics, which sparked Maria's interest in these subjects from a young age. He was also the director of two Warsaw secondary schools for boys. Even though laboratory instruction was removed from Polish schools by Russian authorities, Maria's father didn't let that stop him. He brought laboratory equipment home and taught Maria and her siblings how to use it.

However, life was not easy for the Skłodowski family. Władysław was eventually dismissed from his teaching position due to his pro-Polish sentiments, and the family faced financial difficulties. To make ends meet, they took in boarders to supplement their income.

Maria's mother, Bronisława, had been a headmistress of a prestigious boarding school for girls in Warsaw. She resigned from her position after Maria was born. Tragically, Maria's mother passed away when Maria was only ten years old, succumbing to tuberculosis. Just a few years earlier, Maria's older sister Zofia had also died from typhus.

Despite the challenges and tragedies, Maria's childhood was filled with curiosity and a thirst for knowledge. Little did she know that her early struggles and love for science would pave the way for groundbreaking discoveries in the future.

ERIC LYLANI

Path to Education and Early Challenges

When Maria was ten years old, she started attending a boarding school run by J. Sikorska. Later, she moved to a gymnasium (a type of school) for girls, where she worked hard and graduated with top honors on June 12, 1883, earning a prestigious gold medal for her academic achievements.

After graduation, Maria faced a difficult time. She experienced a collapse, possibly due to feeling very sad and overwhelmed (what we might call depression today). To help her recover, she spent a year in the countryside with relatives of her father. The next year, she returned to Warsaw to be with her father and started tutoring to earn money.

Maria wanted to continue her education and study at a university, but she faced a big problem because she was a woman. At that time, it was very challenging for women to enroll in universities. However, Maria and her sister Bronisława found a clever way to continue their studies. They joined a secret university called the Flying University (also known as the Floating University), which was a special school that accepted women students. This university was not allowed by the Russian authorities, so it operated secretly.

To support her sister's dream of becoming a doctor, Maria made a deal with Bronisława. Maria would work and help financially support Bronisława's medical studies in

Paris, and in return, Bronisława would do the same for Maria two years later.

To earn money for her part of the deal, Maria took different jobs. First, she worked as a home tutor in Warsaw. Later, she spent two years as a governess with a wealthy family in Szczuki.

ERIC LYLANI

Marie's Journey to Paris and Pursuit of Education

At the start of 1890, Maria's sister Bronisława, who had recently married Kazimierz Dłuski, invited Maria to join them in Paris. Maria was excited about the idea of going to Paris, but she faced a big challenge—she couldn't afford the tuition fees for university. It would take her another year and a half to save up enough money.

Maria didn't give up. She was determined to continue her education and pursue her dreams. Her father came to her aid by finding a better-paying job, which helped Maria gather the money she needed.

During this time, Maria didn't stop learning. She spent hours reading books, exchanging letters with intellectuals, and receiving tutoring. She was always eager to soak up knowledge and expand her mind.

In early 1889, Maria returned home to Warsaw to be with her father. She continued working as a governess to support herself financially. However, she didn't let her job stop her from pursuing her passion for science. Maria studied at the Flying University, a secret school that allowed women to learn subjects like math and science.

Maria also began her practical scientific training in a chemistry laboratory at the Museum of Industry and Agriculture on Krakowskie Przedmieście 66, near Warsaw's Old Town. This laboratory was managed by her cousin Józef Boguski, who had worked as an assistant to the famous Russian chemist Dmitri Mendeleyev.

In the laboratory, Maria's curiosity and determination shone brightly. She eagerly conducted experiments and learned essential skills that would prepare her for future discoveries. Maria's journey was filled with challenges, but her love for science and her relentless spirit kept her moving forward.

ERIC LYLANI

Marie's Adventure in Paris Begins

In late 1891, Maria Skłodowska packed her bags and left her home in Poland to start a new chapter of her life in France. When she arrived in Paris, she was welcomed by her sister Bronisława and her brother-in-law Kazimierz Dłuski. They provided her with a temporary place to stay until Marie could find her own place closer to the university.

Maria, now going by the French version of her name, Marie, soon found a small attic apartment in the Latin Quarter, not far from the university where she would continue her studies. She enrolled at the

University of Paris with a determination to learn about physics, chemistry, and mathematics.

Life in Paris was not easy for Marie. She had very little money and had to live on a tight budget. To keep warm during cold winters, she wore all the clothes she had. Marie was so focused on her studies that sometimes she forgot to eat!

During the day, Marie attended classes and conducted experiments. In the evenings, she worked as a tutor to earn enough money to support herself. It was hard work, but Marie was determined to succeed.

In 1893, Marie achieved a major milestone—she earned her degree in physics. She also began working in an industrial laboratory under Gabriel Lippmann. Despite her busy schedule, Marie continued studying at the University of Paris and received a fellowship that allowed her to earn a second degree in 1894.

Marie's scientific journey truly began in Paris. She started by studying the magnetic properties of different types of steel, which was a project commissioned by the Society for the Encouragement of National Industry.

It was during this time that Marie's path crossed with Pierre Curie, a fellow scientist who shared her passion for the natural sciences. Pierre was a teacher at the City of Paris Industrial Physics and Chemistry Higher Educational Institution (ESPCI Paris). They were introduced by a Polish physicist named Józef Wierusz-Kowalski, who knew that Marie needed more space to conduct her experiments.

Although Pierre didn't have a large laboratory, he managed to find some space for Marie to work. This marked the beginning of a remarkable partnership that would lead to groundbreaking discoveries in the field of science.

A Scientific Love Story

Marie Skłodowska and Pierre Curie shared a deep love for science, and this common passion brought them closer together each day. As they worked side by side, studying and conducting experiments, they began to develop special feelings for each other. Pierre eventually asked Marie to marry him.

At first, Marie was hesitant to accept Pierre's proposal because she still had plans to return to her native Poland. However, Pierre was determined to be with her and declared that he would move to Poland with her, even if it meant giving up his career to teach French.

During the summer break of 1894, Marie returned to Warsaw to visit her family. She hoped to continue her scientific work in Poland, but she faced disappointment when she was denied a place at Kraków University due to sexism in academia. Despite this setback, Pierre's heartfelt letter convinced Marie to return to Paris and pursue her dream of earning a PhD.

Pierre, at Marie's insistence, also pursued his own doctoral studies and completed his research on magnetism, earning his own doctorate in March 1895. He was promoted to professor at the School, showing his dedication and support for Marie's ambitions.

On July 26, 1895, Marie and Pierre were married in Sceaux. Marie wore a dark blue outfit instead of a traditional bridal gown, which she would later use as her laboratory outfit for many years.

Marie and Pierre shared many interests outside of science, including long bicycle trips and travels abroad. These experiences strengthened their bond and brought them even closer together. In Pierre, Marie not only found a new love and partner but also a scientific collaborator whom she could depend on.

Together, Marie and Pierre embarked on a remarkable journey of love and discovery, laying the foundation for groundbreaking achievements in the world of science. Their story is a testament to the power of passion, dedication, and partnership.

ERIC LYLANI

Marie Curie's Discoveries and Challenges

In 1895, a scientist named Wilhelm Röntgen discovered something amazing called X-rays. Although people knew about X-rays, they didn't understand how they worked. Then, in 1896, another scientist named Henri Becquerel found out that uranium salts could give off rays similar to X-rays. What was fascinating about this discovery was that these rays seemed to come from uranium all by themselves, without needing any outside source of energy.

Marie Curie was intrigued by these discoveries. Inspired by Röntgen and Becquerel, she decided to make uranium rays the focus of her research for her thesis. Marie used a clever technique to study samples. Her husband Pierre and his brother had invented a sensitive device called an electrometer, which Marie used to discover that uranium rays made the air around a sample conduct electricity.

Marie's first important finding was that the strength of uranium's radiation depended only on how much uranium was present. This led her to think that the radiation came directly from the uranium atom itself, not from interactions between molecules. This idea was a big step in proving that atoms were not just tiny, unchangeable balls, as many scientists had thought.

In the midst of her groundbreaking research, Marie also became a mother. In 1897, she welcomed her daughter Irène into the world. To support her family and continue her scientific work, Marie began teaching at the École Normale Supérieure.

Marie and Pierre didn't have a fancy laboratory for their experiments. Most of their research was done in a converted shed next to ESPCI (City of Paris Industrial Physics and Chemistry Higher Educational Institution). This shed used to be a dissecting room for medical students and was not very comfortable. It was poorly ventilated and not even waterproof!

Unfortunately, during their research with radioactive substances, Marie and Pierre didn't realize the dangerous effects of radiation exposure. They worked without protection, which later led to health problems. Despite these challenges, Marie received financial support for her research from metallurgical and mining companies, as well as from various organizations and governments.

Marie Curie's determination and innovation led her to groundbreaking discoveries, paving the way for our understanding of radiation and the structure of atoms. Her story shows us that great achievements often come from hard work and curiosity, even in the face of challenges.

Marie's Quest for Discovery

Marie Curie was determined to uncover the secrets of radioactive minerals like pitchblende and torbernite. Using her electrometer, Marie discovered that pitchblende was much more active than pure uranium, and torbernite was twice as active. This led her to believe that these minerals contained small amounts of a substance even more powerful than uranium.

Marie embarked on a systematic search for this mysterious substance. In 1898, she made another incredible discovery—she found that the element thorium was also radioactive. Her husband, Pierre Curie, became increasingly fascinated by her work and decided to join her in her research.

The idea to investigate these radioactive minerals was Marie's own. She formulated the research plan herself and sought Pierre's opinion, clearly establishing her ownership of the project. Marie was aware of the challenges she faced as a woman in science, knowing that many scientists might doubt her capabilities.

Understanding the importance of promptly sharing her discoveries, Marie wasted no time in publishing her findings. Just like Becquerel had presented his discovery to the Académie des Sciences soon after making it, Marie quickly submitted her paper to the academy with the help of her former professor, Gabriel Lippmann.

However, Marie faced a setback when she discovered that another scientist, Gerhard Carl Schmidt, had published similar findings two months earlier. Despite this, Marie's paper included a critical observation—that pitchblende and torbernite might contain an element far more active than uranium.

Filled with passion and determination, Marie and Pierre set out to verify their hypothesis. On April 14, 1898, they eagerly began experimenting with a sample of pitchblende, not realizing that the substance they sought was present in incredibly tiny amounts. This marked the beginning of their remarkable journey towards uncovering one of the most significant discoveries in the history of science.

ERIC LYLANI

Marie and Pierre's Remarkable Discoveries

In July 1898, Marie and Pierre Curie made an extraordinary announcement—they had discovered a new element, which they named "polonium" in honor of Marie's native Poland. At that time, Poland was divided among three empires (Russian, Austrian, and Prussian), and naming the element after her homeland held special significance.

Later that year, on December 26, 1898, the Curies unveiled yet another groundbreaking discovery—the element they named "radium," derived from the Latin word for "ray." These discoveries marked significant milestones in the study of radioactivity.

To confirm their discoveries, Marie and Pierre worked tirelessly to isolate polonium and radium in their pure forms. This was no easy task, especially with pitchblende—a complex mineral that required careful chemical separation. Polonium was relatively easier to isolate because it resembled bismuth, a more distinct element in the ore. However, radium proved to be more challenging, as it chemically resembled barium, which also existed in pitchblende.

By 1898, the Curies had obtained traces of radium, but they struggled to isolate appreciable quantities free from contamination with barium. The process of separating radium salt through differential crystallization was arduous. It wasn't until 1902 that they managed to isolate a tiny amount of radium chloride from a tonne of pitchblende. Marie eventually succeeded in isolating pure radium metal in 1910.

Although polonium has a short half-life and could not be isolated in pure form, the Curies' discoveries revolutionized the scientific community. Between 1898 and 1902, they published a remarkable total of 32 scientific papers, demonstrating their dedication to advancing our understanding of radioactivity.

In 1900, Marie Curie made history by becoming the first female faculty member at the École Normale Supérieure, while Pierre joined the faculty of the University of Paris. Despite her achievements, Marie faced challenges as a woman in science. In 1902, she visited Poland upon her father's passing.

In June 1903, under the supervision of Gabriel Lippmann, Marie was awarded her doctorate from the University of Paris. That same month, the Curies were invited to the Royal Institution in London to discuss radioactivity. However, due to societal norms, Marie was not allowed to speak—the honor was given solely to Pierre.

Meanwhile, their discoveries sparked a new industry centered on radium, although the Curies themselves did not patent their findings and did not profit significantly from the growing business.

A Nobel Prize and Tragic Loss

In December 1903, something extraordinary happened—Marie Curie, along with her husband Pierre Curie and Henri Becquerel, received the Nobel Prize in Physics! They were honored for their groundbreaking research on radiation, which all started with Henri Becquerel's initial discovery. Marie made history as the first woman ever to win a Nobel Prize.

Originally, the Nobel committee planned to award the prize only to Pierre Curie and Henri Becquerel. However, thanks to a mathematician named Magnus Gösta Mittag-Leffler, who advocated for women in science, Pierre was alerted to the oversight. After Pierre complained, Marie's name was rightfully added to the nomination.

Despite their remarkable achievement, Marie and Pierre decided not to travel to Stockholm to receive the prize in person. They were deeply engrossed in their scientific work, and Pierre, who disliked public events, was also feeling unwell.

Eventually, in 1905, the Curies made the trip to Stockholm to fulfill their duties as Nobel laureates. The prize money allowed them to hire their first laboratory assistant, further advancing their research efforts.

After winning the Nobel Prize and receiving an offer from the University of Geneva, Pierre was finally offered a professorship at the University of Paris. However, they still didn't have a proper laboratory. Pierre's persistence paid off when the University of Paris agreed to provide a new laboratory, set to be ready by 1906.

In December 1904, Marie gave birth to their second daughter, Ève. Despite her busy schedule, Marie made sure her daughters learned her native language, Polish, hiring Polish governesses to teach them and taking them on visits to Poland.

Tragedy struck on April 19, 1906, when Pierre Curie was killed in a terrible accident. While crossing a street in heavy rain, he was struck by a horse-drawn vehicle and tragically lost his life. Marie was devastated by the loss of her beloved husband.

Despite her grief, Marie was determined to continue Pierre's legacy. On May 13, 1906, the physics department at the University of Paris decided to retain the chair created for Pierre and offer it to Marie. She accepted this role, hoping to establish a world-class laboratory in honor of Pierre.

Marie Curie became the first woman to become a professor at the University of Paris, demonstrating her resilience and commitment to scientific excellence in the face of adversity. Her story continues to inspire countless individuals around the world to pursue their passions and push the boundaries of knowledge.

The Radium Institute and Challenges

Marie Curie's determination to create a state-of-the-art laboratory didn't stop with the University of Paris. As she entered the later years of her scientific career, she took on the leadership of the Radium Institute (Institut du Radium, now Curie Institute, Institut Curie), a specialized radioactivity laboratory established for her by the Pasteur Institute and the University of Paris.

The idea for the Radium Institute came in 1909 from Pierre Paul Émile Roux, director of the Pasteur Institute, who was disappointed by the lack of support from the

University of Paris and suggested that Marie move her research to the Pasteur Institute. Only when faced with the prospect of Marie leaving did the University of Paris finally agree, and the Curie Pavilion became a collaborative effort between the university and the Pasteur Institute.

In 1910, Marie achieved a significant milestone—she successfully isolated radium. She also defined an international standard for measuring radioactive emissions, which was later named after her and Pierre: the curie. Despite these achievements, Marie faced challenges within the scientific community.

In 1911, the French Academy of Sciences narrowly failed to elect Marie Curie as a member, with only one or two votes making the difference. Instead, Édouard Branly, an inventor involved in wireless telegraphy, was elected. This outcome reflected the biases and attitudes prevailing at the time.

Marie Curie's fame as a foreign scientist working in France was overshadowed by xenophobia and false speculation about her background. The press portrayed her negatively during the French Academy of Sciences elections, labeling her as a foreigner.

Upon returning from a conference in Belgium, Marie found herself confronted by an angry mob outside her house and had to seek refuge with her daughters at her friend Camille Marbo's home.

ERIC LYLANI

Continued Recognition and Challenges

Despite facing personal challenges and opposition, Marie Curie's international recognition soared to new heights. In 1911, the Royal Swedish Academy of Sciences honored her once again, this time with the Nobel Prize in Chemistry. This prestigious award acknowledged her outstanding contributions to chemistry through the discovery of radium and polonium, as well as her pioneering work in isolating radium and studying its properties.

However, Marie encountered obstacles related to her personal life. Svante

Arrhenius, the chair of the Nobel committee, initially tried to prevent her from attending the official ceremony for her Nobel Prize in Chemistry due to negative publicity. Marie firmly asserted that her scientific achievements were separate from her private life and insisted on attending the ceremony.

Marie Curie's achievement of winning two Nobel Prizes was unprecedented. She was the first person to accomplish this remarkable feat and remains among a select few Nobel laureates, alongside Linus Pauling, to have received Nobel Prizes in two distinct fields.

Amid growing international acclaim, a delegation of prominent Polish intellectuals, led by renowned novelist Henryk Sienkiewicz, urged Marie to return to Poland and continue her research in her native country. Marie's second Nobel Prize bolstered her efforts to persuade the French government to support the construction of the Radium Institute, which was completed in 1914. This institute became a hub for cutting-edge research in chemistry, physics, and medicine.

Despite her success, Marie faced personal struggles. After accepting her Nobel Prize in 1911, she experienced health issues, including depression and a kidney ailment, which required hospitalization. For most of 1912, she retreated from public life and sought solace in England with her friend and fellow physicist, Hertha Ayrton. Marie returned to her laboratory in December 1912, following a hiatus of about 14 months.

In 1912, the Warsaw Scientific Society offered Marie the directorship of a new laboratory in Warsaw, but she declined in order to focus on developing the Radium Institute in Paris, scheduled for completion in August 1914. Marie was appointed director of the Curie Laboratory within the Radium Institute.

Marie Curie visited Poland in 1913 and was warmly welcomed in Warsaw, although the Russian authorities largely overlooked her visit. The outbreak of World War I interrupted the institute's progress, as many researchers were drafted into the French Army. However, activities at the institute resumed fully in 1919.

Heroism During World War I

During World War I, Marie Curie recognized the urgent need to provide medical care to wounded soldiers on the front lines. She believed that injured soldiers had the best chance of recovery if they were operated on quickly. Marie saw an opportunity to use X-rays to assist battlefield surgeons and to prevent unnecessary amputations.

To help in this effort, Marie quickly learned about radiology, anatomy, and automotive mechanics. She obtained X-ray equipment, vehicles, and auxiliary generators and developed mobile radiography units called "Petites Curies" or "Little Curies." Marie became the director of the Red Cross Radiology Service and established France's first military radiology center, which was operational by late 1914.

With the assistance of a military doctor and her 17-year-old daughter Irène, Marie oversaw the installation of 20 mobile radiological vehicles and 200 radiological units at field hospitals within the first year of the war. Later, she began training other women to assist in radiology.

In 1915, Marie Curie used her own supply of radium to produce hollow needles containing "radium emanation," a radioactive gas later identified as radon. These needles were used for sterilizing infected tissue in wounded soldiers.

It is estimated that over a million wounded soldiers were treated with Marie's X-ray units during the war. Despite her significant contributions to the French war effort, Marie never received formal recognition from the French government for her heroic efforts.

Marie Curie also attempted to donate her Nobel Prize medals to support the war effort, but the French National Bank refused to accept them. Instead, she used her Nobel Prize money to purchase war bonds, believing that her resources could better serve the needs of her country during the war.

Marie was actively involved in committees dedicated to the Polish cause in France and remained committed to supporting her homeland. After the war, she documented her experiences in a book titled "Radiology in War" (1919), summarizing the critical role of radiology in providing medical care during wartime.

Marie Curie's dedication, ingenuity, and selflessness during World War I exemplify her unwavering commitment to advancing science and serving humanity, even in the face of adversity and challenges. Her contributions saved countless lives and continue to inspire generations of scientists and humanitarians around the world.

Marie Curie's Continued Impact and Achievements

In 1920, the French government honored Marie Curie on the 25th anniversary of her discovery of radium by establishing a special stipend for her. This honor had previously been held by Louis Pasteur, a renowned scientist who passed away in 1895.

The following year, Marie Curie embarked on a triumphant tour of the United States to raise funds for radium research. Mrs. William Brown Meloney, who interviewed Marie Curie, created the Marie Curie Radium Fund and successfully raised money to purchase radium, drawing attention to Marie's important work.

During her visit to the United States, Marie Curie was received by U.S. President Warren G. Harding at the White House. She was presented with 1 gram of radium collected in the United States, and the First Lady praised her as a role model for professional achievement and as a supportive wife.

As Marie's fame grew internationally, the French government offered her the Legion of Honour award, but she declined this official distinction. Instead, in 1922, she became a fellow of the French Academy of Medicine.

Marie Curie continued to travel extensively, visiting countries like Belgium, Brazil, Spain, and Czechoslovakia to share her knowledge through public appearances and lectures.

Under Marie Curie's leadership, the Institute she founded produced four more Nobel Prize winners, including her daughter, Irène Joliot-Curie, and her son-in-law, Frédéric Joliot-Curie. Over time, this institute became one of the world's leading centers for research on radioactivity, alongside other prestigious laboratories in Europe.

In August 1922, Marie Curie joined the League of Nations' International Committee on Intellectual Cooperation, contributing to scientific coordination alongside prominent researchers like Albert Einstein and Henri Bergson.

Marie Curie's efforts extended to writing a biography of her late husband, Pierre Curie, in 1923. She also played a key role in laying the foundations for the Warsaw Radium Institute during her visit to Poland in 1925.

Her second American tour in 1929 successfully equipped the Warsaw Radium Institute with radium, and the institute officially opened its doors in 1932 with Marie's sister Bronisława as its director.

Despite the distractions caused by her public engagements and the associated publicity, Marie Curie's efforts provided crucial resources for her scientific work. They enabled important advancements in the field of radioactivity.

In recognition of her contributions, Marie Curie was awarded the Cameron Prize for

Therapeutics by the University of Edinburgh in 1931, underscoring her enduring impact on science and medicine.

ERIC LYLANI

Marie Curie's Legacy and Passing

Marie Curie made her final visit to Poland in early 1934, bidding farewell to her homeland. A few months later, on July 4, 1934, she passed away at the Sancellemoz sanatorium in Passy, Haute-Savoie, at the age of 66. The cause of her death was aplastic anemia, believed to be linked to her prolonged exposure to radiation during her groundbreaking research.

During Marie Curie's lifetime, the harmful effects of ionizing radiation were not fully understood, and safety measures were not as advanced as they are today. She often carried test tubes containing radioactive isotopes in her pocket and stored them in her desk drawer, noting the faint glow emitted by these substances in the dark.

Marie Curie's exposure to X-rays while serving as a radiologist in field hospitals during World War I further contributed to her health challenges later in life. However, when her body was examined in 1995, experts concluded that the levels of radium she had been exposed to during her lifetime were unlikely to have been directly responsible for her illness. Instead, it was suggested that her work with radiography during the war may have played a larger role.

Marie Curie was laid to rest beside her beloved husband, Pierre Curie, at the cemetery in Sceaux. Sixty years later, in 1995, both Marie and Pierre Curie were honored for their extraordinary achievements when their remains were transferred to the Paris Panthéon. Their final resting places are sealed in lead-lined tombs due to their high levels of radioactivity.

Marie Curie's papers from the 1890s, including her cookbooks, remain highly radioactive and are stored in special lead-lined containers. Researchers who wish to study her work must wear protective clothing to shield themselves from the radiation.

In her last year, Marie Curie worked on a book titled "Radioactivity," which was published posthumously in 1935. Her legacy continues to inspire scientists and researchers around the world, and she remains a symbol of dedication, perseverance, and groundbreaking discovery in the field of science.

ERIC LYLANI

Marie Curie's Lasting Impact

Marie Curie's groundbreaking work alongside her husband, Pierre, had a profound effect on the twentieth and twenty-first centuries, shaping both the scientific landscape and societal perceptions.

Their discovery of radium's intense radioactivity was truly revolutionary. Radium's properties challenged existing principles in physics and led to a reevaluation of the fundamental laws governing energy conservation. Scientists like Ernest Rutherford used radium's radioactivity to delve into the structure of the atom, leading to the postulation of the nuclear atom model.

In medicine, the discovery of radium offered new hope in the fight against cancer. The ability of radium to emit radiation became a promising avenue for treating cancerous cells.

Marie Curie's journey was not only scientific but also deeply personal. As a woman in a male-dominated field, she faced numerous obstacles in both her native Poland and her adopted country, France. Despite these challenges, she demonstrated remarkable perseverance, breaking through barriers to achieve scientific acclaim.

Marie Curie was admired for her integrity and modest lifestyle. She exhibited remarkable generosity, returning a scholarship she received once she began earning and sharing her Nobel Prize money with friends, family, and colleagues.

An unusual decision was her choice not to patent the process for isolating radium. By forgoing personal gain, she ensured that the scientific community could freely explore and build upon her discoveries.

Throughout her life, Marie Curie remained humble, often refusing awards and medals. Even famed scientist Albert Einstein acknowledged her unwavering dedication to science, remarking that she was likely immune to the corrupting influences of fame.

Marie Curie's legacy continues to inspire generations of scientists, particularly women, to pursue their passions and push boundaries in the pursuit of knowledge. Her impact on science and society endures as a testament to the power of dedication, courage, and scientific curiosity.

ERIC LYLANI

A Legacy of Inspiration

Marie Curie's remarkable contributions to science have earned her a place in history as an iconic figure celebrated around the world, including in popular culture.

She was a trailblazer, breaking barriers and achieving numerous firsts in the world of science. Marie Curie was not only the first woman to win a Nobel Prize but also the first person ever to win two Nobel Prizes in two different scientific fields!

Marie Curie's achievements have been honored with a multitude of awards, medals, and even prestigious honors, like having elements and units of measurement named after her. For instance, the unit of radioactivity, the "curie," is named after Marie and her husband Pierre.

Entities and institutions across the globe proudly bear her name, from universities like Maria Skłodowska-Curie University in Poland to schools and research institutes dedicated to science education and research.

Marie Curie's life has also inspired numerous biographies, books, and films that celebrate her groundbreaking work and perseverance in the face of challenges. Talented actors have portrayed her on screen, ensuring that her legacy continues to inspire new generations.

Marie Curie's image has been featured on postage stamps, banknotes, and even coins, highlighting her enduring impact on science and society.

Her story serves as a powerful reminder that anyone, regardless of background or gender, can make a significant impact through dedication, hard work, and a passion for discovery. Marie Curie's legacy continues to inspire scientists and innovators around the world to reach for the stars and push the boundaries of knowledge.

ERIC LYLANI

Influence on Women's Rights

Marie Curie's life story is not just about science; it's also about breaking down barriers for women. In her time, many people thought women couldn't be scientists or professors. But Marie didn't let that stop her.

Marie Curie showed everyone that women are just as smart and capable as men. She studied hard and became one of the first women to earn a degree in physics. Later, she went on to make groundbreaking discoveries in radioactivity with her husband, Pierre Curie.

Marie faced a lot of challenges because of her gender. People doubted her abilities and questioned whether she belonged in the world of science. But Marie never gave up. She worked tirelessly to prove herself and her worth.

One of Marie's biggest contributions to women's rights was simply by being herself— a determined and brilliant scientist who didn't let anyone tell her what she couldn't do. Her success opened doors for other women who wanted to pursue careers in science and academia.

Marie Curie's story teaches us that anyone, regardless of gender, can achieve greatness with hard work, determination, and belief in themselves. She continues to inspire girls and women everywhere to follow their dreams and break down barriers, just like she did.

Impact on Medicine

Marie Curie's discoveries didn't just change the world of science; they also revolutionized medicine, especially in the fight against cancer.

Marie's groundbreaking work with radioactive elements like radium and polonium led to the development of new ways to treat diseases. One of the most significant applications of her discoveries was in the field of oncology, which focuses on understanding and treating cancer.

The use of radiation in medicine began with Marie Curie's research. She discovered that radiation emitted by radium and other radioactive substances could penetrate living tissue. This discovery laid the foundation for radiation therapy, a crucial treatment method for cancer.

In the early days of radiation therapy, doctors used radioactive substances to target and destroy cancer cells. This treatment method became known as radiotherapy. Marie Curie's work paved the way for advancements in this field, which have saved countless lives over the years.

Today, radiation therapy is a common and effective treatment for many types of cancer. It's used alongside surgery and chemotherapy to shrink tumors and eliminate cancer cells. The techniques and principles developed from Marie Curie's discoveries continue to be refined and improved by scientists and medical professionals around the world.

Marie Curie's impact on medicine extends far beyond her lifetime. Her dedication to scientific discovery has had a lasting effect on how we understand and treat diseases like cancer, demonstrating the immense value of her pioneering research.

ERIC LYLANI

Educational Legacy

Marie Curie not only made groundbreaking discoveries in science but also left behind a powerful legacy in education. Her contributions continue to inspire and empower generations of scientists, especially women in STEM (Science, Technology, Engineering, and Mathematics) fields.

Marie faced many challenges as a woman pursuing higher education and a career in science. Despite these obstacles, she persevered and became the first woman to win a Nobel Prize and the only person to win

Nobel Prizes in two different scientific fields.

Marie's achievements opened doors for women in science, showing that gender should not limit anyone's aspirations or potential. She believed in the importance of education and encouraged young people, especially girls, to pursue their interests in science and discovery.

Marie Curie's story continues to motivate students around the world. Her passion for learning and dedication to scientific research inspire future scientists to explore new ideas and push the boundaries of knowledge.

Marie's educational legacy lives on through initiatives that support women in STEM fields and encourage diversity in scientific research. Many schools, universities, and organizations offer scholarships, programs, and resources to empower young women interested in pursuing careers in science.

Marie Curie's life serves as a reminder that curiosity, perseverance, and a love for learning can lead to incredible discoveries and change the world. Her impact on education continues to shape the future of science and inspire the next generation of innovators and problem-solvers.

ERIC LYLANI

Philosophical Views

Marie Curie was not only a brilliant scientist but also a thinker who pondered deeply about the nature of science, discovery, and the pursuit of knowledge.

Marie believed that science was a powerful tool for understanding the world around us. She was fascinated by the mysteries of nature and dedicated her life to unraveling them through rigorous experimentation and research.

To Marie, discovery was not just about finding answers but also about asking the right questions. She believed in the importance of curiosity and persistence in scientific inquiry. For her, the pursuit of knowledge was a lifelong journey filled with excitement and wonder.

Marie's work with radioactive elements like radium and polonium led her to contemplate the fundamental properties of matter and energy. She contributed to the transformation of scientific understanding, challenging established beliefs and pushing the boundaries of human knowledge.

One of Marie's most enduring philosophical views was that science should be a force for good in the world. She envisioned that her discoveries could improve human health and advance medical treatments. Marie advocated for the responsible use of scientific knowledge for the benefit of society.

Marie Curie's philosophical outlook on science emphasized the importance of integrity, perseverance, and the ethical responsibility of scientists. She believed in the power of education to inspire future generations and ignite a passion for discovery.

ERIC LYLANI

Marie Curie's Enduring Influence

Marie Curie's groundbreaking discoveries continue to shape modern scientific research and innovation in significant ways.

Marie's work in understanding radioactivity laid the groundwork for critical advancements in medicine. Her discovery of radium's properties led to the development of radiotherapy, a vital treatment for cancer that targets and destroys cancerous cells.

Moreover, Marie Curie's research in radioactivity contributed to the understanding of nuclear physics, which underpins the generation of nuclear energy used to produce electricity worldwide.

The principles of radioactivity she uncovered have also found applications in various industries. Radioactive isotopes are used in agriculture, food safety, environmental monitoring, and geological exploration, benefiting society in diverse ways.

Marie Curie's life story and achievements continue to inspire future scientists, especially women in STEM fields. By breaking barriers in science and demonstrating the power of determination and curiosity, she encourages aspiring researchers to pursue their passions and contribute to scientific progress.

Beyond her scientific contributions, Marie Curie's ethical approach to scientific inquiry serves as a lasting legacy. Her dedication to responsible research and the thoughtful application of scientific knowledge sets a precedent for ethical conduct in the scientific community.

Marie Curie's enduring influence is a testament to the transformative impact of scientific discovery and the enduring legacy of a pioneering scientist who changed the course of history with her work.

ERIC LYLANI

Marie Curie's Scientific Method

Marie Curie's approach to science was marked by dedication, curiosity, and meticulous attention to detail. Her scientific method was a key factor in her groundbreaking discoveries.

Marie approached her experiments with a curious and questioning mind. She wanted to understand the mysteries of nature, particularly the properties of radiation.

In her laboratory, Marie conducted careful and systematic investigations. She followed strict protocols and procedures to ensure accuracy and reliability in her findings.

Marie was known for her persistence and perseverance. She would repeat experiments multiple times to verify results and eliminate any sources of error.

Her methodical approach included recording detailed observations and data. Marie believed in the importance of precise measurements and thorough documentation.

Marie's scientific method involved collaboration with her husband, Pierre Curie, and other researchers. They shared ideas, discussed findings, and collectively pursued scientific breakthroughs.

Hobbies and Interests

Marie Curie, the brilliant scientist known for her discoveries in radioactivity, had many hobbies and interests outside of her scientific work. Despite her dedication to research, Marie found joy in various activities that brought balance to her life.

One of Marie Curie's favorite hobbies was reading. She had a great love for books and spent many hours immersed in literature. Marie particularly enjoyed reading about science, mathematics, and philosophy. Her curiosity extended beyond the laboratory, and she often explored complex ideas and theories through books.

Marie was also passionate about spending time outdoors. She appreciated nature and found solace in walks through parks and gardens. The fresh air and beauty of the natural world provided her with inspiration and relaxation amidst her busy scientific pursuits.

Another interest of Marie's was teaching and mentoring. She was dedicated to educating others, especially young students interested in science. Marie believed strongly in the importance of education and enjoyed sharing her knowledge and passion for discovery with others.

Marie Curie was also known for her humanitarian efforts. She volunteered her time to help wounded soldiers during World War I, using her scientific expertise to develop mobile X-ray units that could be used on the battlefield. Her compassion and commitment to helping others extended beyond the laboratory.

In her leisure time, Marie enjoyed spending quality moments with her family. She cherished her time with her husband Pierre and their two daughters, Irène and Ève. They shared meals together, explored new places, and engaged in meaningful conversations.

Despite her busy life as a scientist, Marie Curie valued a well-rounded lifestyle that included intellectual pursuits, outdoor activities, teaching, humanitarian work, and quality time with loved ones. Her diverse interests and hobbies enriched her life and contributed to her remarkable legacy as a scientist and a compassionate human being.

ERIC LYLANI

Inspiring Her Children's Achievements

Marie Curie was not only a pioneering scientist but also a loving mother to her two daughters, Irène and Ève. Her children grew up surrounded by their mother's passion for science and dedication to discovery, which inspired them to pursue their own remarkable achievements.

Irène Curie, Marie's elder daughter, followed in her parents' footsteps and became a distinguished scientist in her own right. She collaborated with her husband, Frédéric Joliot-Curie, in groundbreaking research on artificial radioactivity, for which they were jointly awarded the Nobel Prize in Chemistry in 1935. Irène's work furthered our understanding of nuclear physics and paved the way for advancements in nuclear medicine.

Irène had a close and supportive relationship with her mother, Marie Curie. They shared a deep bond over their shared passion for science, and Marie encouraged Irène to pursue her scientific interests. Despite the challenges faced by women in science during that time, Marie was a source of inspiration and mentorship for Irène, fostering her daughter's scientific curiosity and ambition.

Ève Curie, Marie's younger daughter, took a different path and became a successful writer and journalist. She authored several books, including a biography of her mother titled "Madame Curie," which became widely acclaimed. Through her writing, Ève celebrated her mother's legacy and contributions to science, ensuring that Marie Curie's story would continue to inspire future generations.

Both Irène and Ève cherished their mother's guidance and support. Marie Curie instilled in her children the values of perseverance, intellectual curiosity, and compassion. Despite the demands of her scientific career, Marie always made time for her family, nurturing a warm and nurturing home environment where her children could thrive.

The close relationship between Marie Curie and her daughters was built on mutual respect and admiration. Marie's determination and resilience in the face of challenges inspired Irène and Ève to pursue their passions and make significant contributions to their respective fields.

ERIC LYLANI

Exploring Marie Curie's Collaborations and Mentors

Marie Curie's remarkable scientific journey was marked by collaborations with fellow scientists and the guidance of mentors who shaped her career and research direction.

Partnership with Pierre Curie

Marie's most important collaboration was with her husband, Pierre Curie, who was already an accomplished physicist when they met. Pierre recognized Marie's brilliance and shared her passion for scientific exploration. Together, they embarked on groundbreaking experiments that led to the discovery of new elements like polonium and radium.

Pierre's support and scientific insight were crucial to Marie's success. Their partnership was a true collaboration, with each contributing unique skills and ideas. Their combined efforts earned them the Nobel Prize in Physics in 1903, recognizing their pioneering work in radioactivity.

Guidance from Henri Becquerel

Another influential figure in Marie's life was Henri Becquerel, the physicist who discovered radioactivity. Becquerel's accidental discovery sparked Marie's interest in the field. Under his mentorship, Marie learned about the properties of radiation and its potential applications.

Becquerel's patient guidance and scientific rigor inspired Marie to conduct her own experiments. His mentorship was instrumental in shaping Marie's research direction and instilling in her a deep curiosity about the mysteries of radioactivity.

Impact of Collaboration and Mentorship

Marie Curie's collaborations with Pierre Curie and mentorship under Henri Becquerel were pivotal in her scientific journey. These experiences taught her the importance of teamwork, meticulous research, and the pursuit of knowledge. They also empowered her to break gender barriers in science and make groundbreaking discoveries that continue to influence modern science.

ERIC LYLANI

Historical Context of Marie Curie's Birth

Marie Curie was born on November 7, 1867, in Warsaw during a period of significant historical and political change in Europe, particularly in Poland. At that time, Poland was under Russian rule as part of the Congress Poland region, which had been partitioned between Russia, Prussia (later part of Germany), and Austria since the late 18th century.

Living under Russian control, the Polish population faced suppression of their cultural and political identity. The Russian Empire imposed restrictions on the Polish language, education, and cultural activities, contributing to a climate of national identity struggle and resistance among the Polish people.

Despite the political challenges, Warsaw, where Marie Curie was born, remained a center of intellectual and cultural activity. Polish intellectuals, artists, and scientists played a vital role in preserving Polish heritage and fostering a sense of national pride and resilience.

Marie Curie's upbringing in this environment had a profound impact on her character and ambitions. Raised in a family that valued education and culture, she developed a strong desire for knowledge and self-improvement from an early age.

The oppressive political climate under Russian rule likely fueled Marie Curie's determination to pursue higher education and contribute to the field of science. Her relentless pursuit of knowledge and scientific achievement reflected her resilience in the face of adversity and her commitment to overcoming obstacles.

Understanding the historical context of Marie Curie's birth helps us appreciate the challenges she faced and the resilience she demonstrated in her pursuit of scientific discovery. Her story serves as a testament to the transformative power of education and determination in overcoming adversity and making lasting contributions to the world.

ERIC LYLANI

The Discovery of Polonium

In July 1898, Marie and Pierre Curie made a groundbreaking discovery while investigating the radioactivity of pitchblende, a type of uranium ore. They isolated a new element from this ore and named it "polonium," after Marie Curie's homeland, Poland. At that time, Poland was not an independent country; it was divided among Russia, Germany, and Austria-Hungary. Naming the element after Poland was a way for Marie Curie to draw attention to her country's lack of independence.

Polonium was the first element discovered by the Curies during their study of pitchblende's radioactivity. They found that even after removing uranium and thorium, the remaining pitchblende was still highly radioactive. This discovery led them to search for other radioactive elements, resulting in the isolation of polonium in July 1898 and radium five months later.

In 1902, German scientist Willy Marckwald independently isolated polonium but believed it to be a new element, which he called "radio-tellurium." It wasn't until 1905 that it was confirmed to be the same element discovered by the Curies.

During World War II, polonium gained significance in the United States as part of the Manhattan Project's Dayton Project. Polonium, along with beryllium, was used as the 'Urchin' initiator of the atomic bomb, ensuring a successful nuclear chain reaction.

This technology was kept classified until the 1960s.

Polonium is a rare, highly radioactive metal with no stable isotopes. Its natural occurrence is limited to tiny traces, such as polonium-210 found in uranium ores. Polonium-210 has a short half-life of 138 days, making longer-lived isotopes like polonium-209 much harder to produce.

Today, polonium is primarily produced in small quantities through neutron irradiation of bismuth. Due to its intense radioactivity, polonium has limited applications, including use in space probe heaters, antistatic devices, neutron sources, and alpha particle sources. However, it is also known for its extreme toxicity to humans, famously used in the poisoning of Alexander Litvinenko.

Marie and Pierre Curie's discovery of polonium marked a significant milestone in the study of radioactivity and the periodic table. Their work not only expanded our understanding of chemical elements but also highlighted the potential dangers and applications of radioactive materials.

The Discovery of Radium

Radium, a remarkable element, was discovered by Marie Skłodowska-Curie and her husband, Pierre Curie, on a chilly day in December 1898. They were conducting experiments on a mineral called pitchblende, trying to understand why it was so radioactive. When they removed uranium from the pitchblende, they realized that the remaining material still possessed strong radioactivity. This surprising observation led them deeper into their investigation.

In July of that same year, while studying pitchblende, they uncovered an element that resembled bismuth. This new element turned out to be polonium, another significant discovery. As they continued their research, they isolated a radioactive mixture with two main components: compounds of barium, which produced a bright green flame, and mysterious radioactive compounds that emitted carmine spectral lines never seen before. These findings were groundbreaking and allowed the Curies to isolate these compounds further, ultimately revealing a new element.

Excited by their discoveries, the Curies shared their findings with the French Academy of Sciences on December 26, 1898, just days after their breakthrough. The element was later named "radium" around 1899, deriving from the French word "radium" linked to "radius," acknowledging radium's unique ability to emit energy in the form of rays.

In September 1910, Marie Curie, alongside André-Louis Debierne, accomplished another significant milestone by isolating radium as a pure metal. They achieved this feat through the electrolysis of pure radium chloride solution using a mercury cathode, resulting in radium-mercury amalgam. By heating this amalgam in a hydrogen gas atmosphere, they successfully removed the mercury, leaving behind pure radium metal.

Industrial production of radium commenced at the beginning of the 20th century in Belgium, thanks to companies like Biraco, a subsidiary of Union Minière du Haut Katanga (UMHK). Radium's impact on science and medicine was profound, leading to the development of units like the curie, which measures radioactivity based on radium-226's properties.

Today, radium remains a critical element in understanding radioactivity and its effects. It is primarily found in uranium and thorium ores, although in trace amounts. Despite its historical uses in radioluminescent devices and medical applications, radium's extreme toxicity has limited its commercial use. Instead, safer isotopes of other elements are now used in modern applications, marking radium's unique journey from discovery to contemporary scientific understanding.

The Dangers of Radioactivity

In the early 1900s, Marie Curie discovered something extraordinary called "radioactivity." Marie loved to study elements and atoms, and her curiosity led her to uncover new elements like radium and polonium. But along with her amazing discoveries, Marie also learned about the hidden dangers of radioactivity.

Radioactivity is like a magic power hidden inside certain elements. It makes them glow and emit special rays that can't be seen with our eyes. Marie and her husband, Pierre, discovered radium—a shiny, glowing metal that fascinated everyone. But what they didn't know at first was that radium, like other radioactive materials, can be very dangerous.

One day, Marie noticed that her skin started to get red and sore from working with radium. She realized that too much exposure to radium's invisible rays could harm her body. This was the first clue that radioactivity could be both powerful and risky.

As Marie continued her research, she discovered that exposure to radioactive materials could cause serious health problems, like making people feel sick or causing their skin to burn. Over time, Marie and other scientists learned that too much exposure to radiation could even lead to very serious illnesses like cancer.

Marie Curie's discoveries helped people understand the dangers of radioactivity. She worked hard to protect herself and others by using special tools and equipment to handle radioactive materials safely. Even though she faced risks, Marie was brave and careful in her work.

Today, scientists use Marie Curie's discoveries to keep us safe from the dangers of radioactivity. They wear special gear and use instruments to measure radiation levels, just like Marie did. This helps them work with radioactive materials without getting hurt.

Remember, just like Marie Curie, it's important to be curious and explore the world around us. But when it comes to things like radioactivity, we must also be cautious and follow safety rules. By learning from Marie's story, we can understand how to use science to make our world better while staying safe and healthy.

The Benefits of Radioactivity

In the world of science, radioactivity has both risks and benefits. It's important to learn about its positive uses and how it has contributed to advancements in medicine and technology.

Radioactivity, discovered by scientists like Marie Curie, has been harnessed for beneficial purposes. One major area is medicine. Radioactive materials are used in treatments for certain cancers. Doctors can target tumors with radiation to help shrink or eliminate them, a technique known as radiation therapy.

Another benefit of radioactivity is in imaging technology. Have you heard of X-rays? They are a type of radiation that can pass through the body, allowing doctors to see inside without surgery. This helps diagnose broken bones or find other health issues.

In industry, radioactivity is used to check the thickness of materials like steel or to detect flaws in metal parts. This ensures that products are made to high standards and are safe for use.

Even in everyday life, radioactivity is present. Smoke detectors often contain a small amount of a radioactive material called americium-241. This helps detect smoke and alert us to potential fires.

It's fascinating how scientists like Marie Curie laid the foundation for using radioactivity in beneficial ways. However, it's essential to handle radioactive materials with care and always follow safety guidelines.

ERIC LYLANI

Lessons from Marie Curie

Marie Curie's life is filled with practical lessons that can inspire us to pursue our dreams and excel in our endeavors. Here's some practical advice distilled from Marie Curie's remarkable journey:

- **Embrace Curiosity:** Cultivate a sense of curiosity about the world around you. Ask questions, seek answers, and explore topics that ignite your interest. Curiosity is the driving force behind scientific discovery and personal growth.

- **Work Hard:** Marie Curie's dedication to her work was unwavering. Success often comes from persistence and hard work. Set ambitious goals for yourself and commit to putting in the effort required to achieve them.

- **Never Give Up**: Marie faced numerous challenges and setbacks throughout her career, but she persevered with determination. When faced with obstacles, adopt a resilient mindset and keep pushing forward towards your goals.

- **Collaborate**: Foster relationships with peers who share your interests and passions. Collaboration can lead to new ideas, innovative solutions, and shared achievements. Learn from others and contribute your unique perspective to joint endeavors.

- **Be Fearless in Innovation**: Don't be afraid to explore unconventional ideas or challenge existing norms. Innovation often requires thinking outside the box and taking calculated risks. Trust your instincts and pursue ideas that have the potential to make a meaningful impact.

- **Set High Standards:** Strive for excellence in everything you do. Set high standards for yourself and hold yourself accountable for achieving them. Continuous improvement and a commitment to quality can lead to outstanding accomplishments.

- **Stay Curious About Learning:** Education is a lifelong journey. Stay curious and continue to expand your knowledge and skills. Explore different subjects and pursue opportunities for growth and development.

- **Seek Inspiration:** Learn from the stories of role models like Marie Curie. Draw inspiration from their achievements and use them as motivation to pursue your own aspirations.

- **Take Care of Yourself:** Success is not just about hard work; it's also about maintaining a healthy balance in life. Prioritize self-care, including physical exercise, mental relaxation, and adequate rest, to sustain your energy and creativity.

- **Believe in Yourself:** Marie Curie's journey is a testament to the power of self-belief. Trust in your abilities, stay focused on your goals and have confidence that you can overcome challenges and achieve great things.

By incorporating these practical lessons into your own life, you can follow in Marie Curie's footsteps and pave the way for your own success.

CONCLUSION

As we reach the end of our journey through the remarkable life of Marie Curie, we are left with a profound sense of awe and admiration for this extraordinary scientist. Marie's story is one of perseverance, passion, and pioneering spirit.

Throughout her life, Marie faced countless challenges and obstacles, yet she never wavered in her pursuit of knowledge and discovery. From her early days in Warsaw, where she defied societal norms to pursue her education, to her groundbreaking research alongside her husband Pierre in

Paris, Marie's journey exemplifies the power of determination and resilience.

Marie Curie's scientific achievements have left an indelible mark on history. Her discoveries of radium and polonium revolutionized our understanding of radioactivity and laid the foundation for advancements in medicine and nuclear science. Marie's unwavering commitment to scientific inquiry and her dedication to improving the world through her research continue to inspire scientists and thinkers around the globe.

Beyond her scientific contributions, Marie Curie's legacy extends to her advocacy for women's rights and education. She shattered glass ceilings and paved the way for future generations of women in STEM fields.

As we reflect on Marie Curie's enduring influence, let us carry forward her spirit of curiosity, courage, and innovation. Let us embrace the challenges before us with determination and optimism, knowing that, like Marie, we too can make a difference in the world.

Marie Curie's life is a testament to the boundless possibilities of the human mind and the transformative power of scientific discovery. Let us honor her legacy by embracing curiosity, pursuing knowledge, and striving to leave a positive impact on the world around us.

Thank you for joining me on this incredible journey through Marie Curie's life and legacy. May her story continue to inspire and empower us all to reach for the stars.

ERIC LYLANI

Made in the USA
Las Vegas, NV
25 November 2024

12603952R00075